T0395180

Silly Joke Books

SILLY JOKES ABOUT MONSTERS

by Michael Dahl

PEBBLE
a capstone imprint

Published by Pebble, an imprint of Capstone
1710 Roe Crest Drive, North Mankato, Minnesota 56003
capstonepub.com

Library of Congress Cataloging-in-Publication Data
Names: Dahl, Michael, author.
Title: Silly jokes about monsters / by Michael Dahl.
Description: North Mankato, Minnesota : Pebble, [2022] | Series: Silly joke books | Audience: Ages: 5-8 | Audience: Grades: 2-3 | Summary: "Get ready to laugh about monsters! These monster jokes will have you telling them again and again; even if you're scared silly! Funny photos combined with hilarious jokes will have young readers laughing out loud"-- Provided by publisher.
Identifiers: LCCN 2021002776 (print) | LCCN 2021002777 (ebook) | ISBN 9781977131614 (hardcover) | ISBN 9781977154866 (pdf) | ISBN 9781977156525 (kindle edition) Subjects: LCSH: Monsters--Juvenile humor. | Wit and humor, Juvenile.
Classification: LCC PN6231.M665 D354 2022 (print) | LCC PN6231.M665 (ebook) | DDC 818/.60208037--dc23
LC record available at https://lccn.loc.gov/2021002776
LC ebook record available at https://lccn.loc.gov/2021002777

Editorial Credits
Editor: Christianne Jones; Designer: Brann Garvey and Mighty Media; Media Researcher: Jo Miller; Production Specialist: Laura Manthe

Image Credits
Shutterstock: Aleksandra Wilert, 12, ice cream cone, alexlibris, 21, book, Andreas Argirakis, 6, cave, Ari N, 15, burger, arjma, 9, background, bibakin, 12, cyclops, Cafe Racer, 19, sunglasses, Elmiraot, Cover, Eric Isselee, 19, gorilla, Fer Gregory, 13, monster, FOTOKITA, 10, ghost, 14, hands, Igor Salov, 6, eyes, Irina Rogova, 18, bows, Luis Louro, 5, girl , Lus Kudritskaya, 24, Marina Kapitu, 23, MaryJane Killinger, 10, toast, Mix and Match Studio, 11, Paradise studio, 4, hands, 9, hands, Peter Albrektsen, 19, truck, posteriori, 15, iceberg, Prokhorovich, 3, Rawpixel.com, 18, ghost, Roman Samborskyi, 20, RUKSUTAKARN studio, 21, wand, 21, SeventyFour, 8, sezer66, 14, dentist, souloff, design element, Suzanne Tucker, 16, Tatiana Popova, 4, deck, 4, hand of cards, Unique Vision, 15, yeti, 21, yeti, Virrage Images, 5, background, zef art, 17

All internet sites appearing in back matter were available and accurate when this book was sent to press.

Printed in the United States   5368

Table of Contents

HELLO!

FUNNY FRIGHTS

Why are mummies always so busy?

They get wrapped up in their work.

What vampire wins every game he plays?

Draculuck.

Why did the zombie lose the card game?

He had a rotten hand.

What building is a vampire
afraid to enter?

A lighthouse.

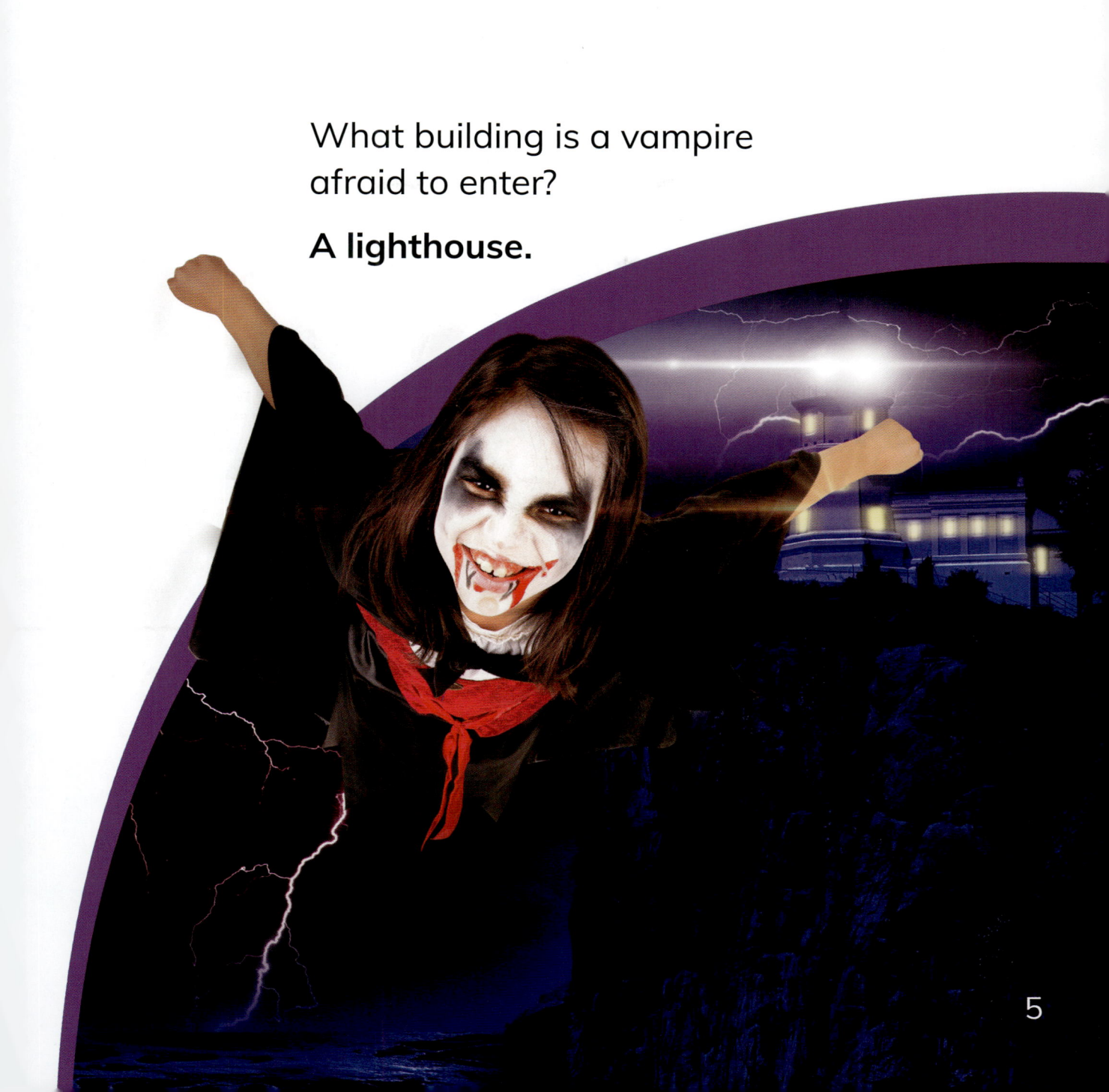

5

RAWRRRR, ZZZZZZ!

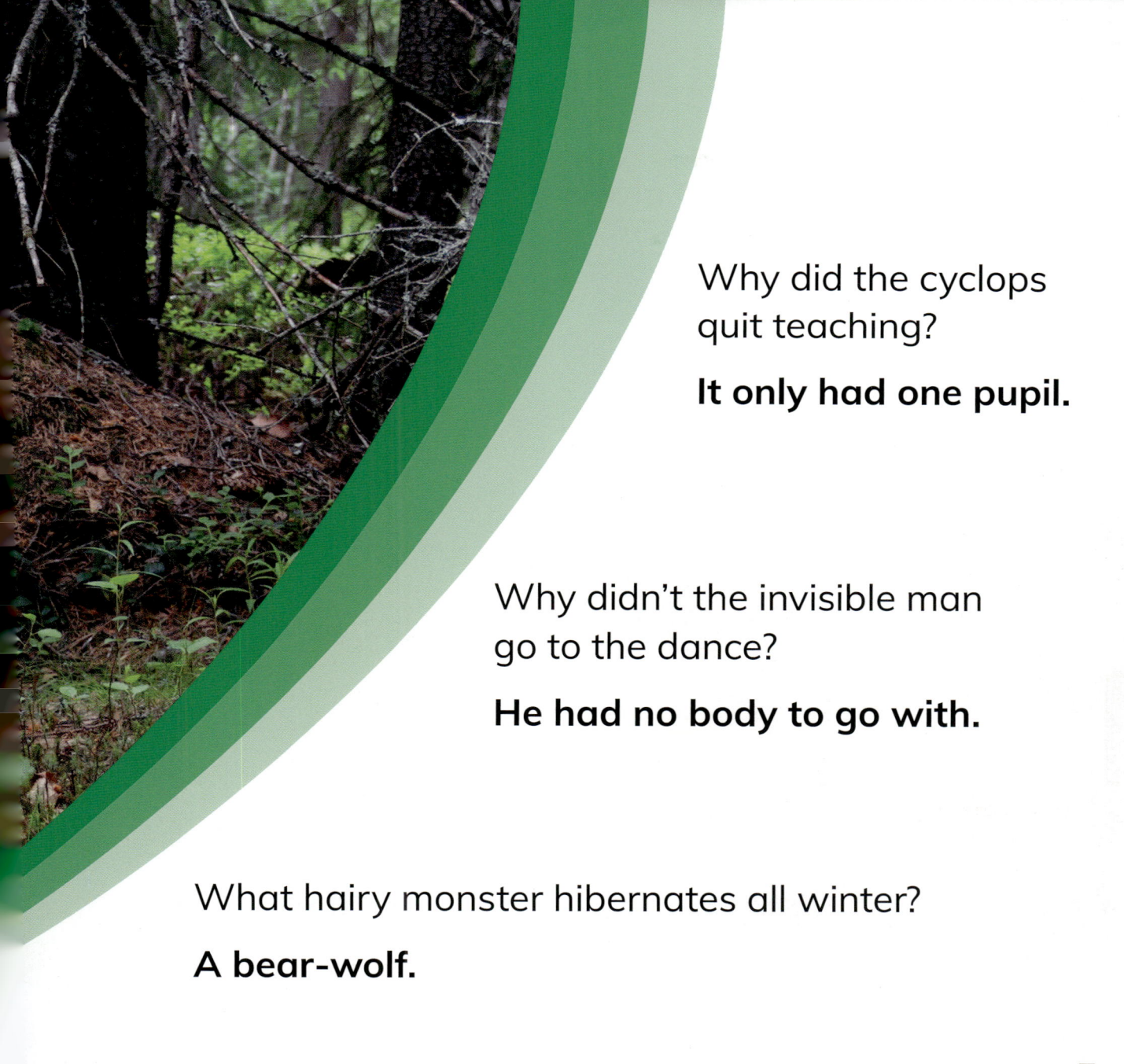

Why did the cyclops
quit teaching?

It only had one pupil.

Why didn't the invisible man
go to the dance?

He had no body to go with.

What hairy monster hibernates all winter?

A bear-wolf.

Where can you always find
a haunted house?

On a dead end.

SHHH!

If zombies
attack, what's
the safest room
in the house?

The living room.

8

Why are the gates at
a cemetery always locked?

Everyone is dying to get in!

What game do werewolves like to play?

Hide-and-shriek!

What keeps a monster cool in the summer?

A scare conditioner.

What do ghosts eat for breakfast?

Ghost toast and booberries.

10

How can you tell a vampire has a cold?

He starts coffin!

11

MONSTER MUNCHIES

How do monsters like their eggs?

Terror-fried.

YUMMY EYES!

What does the cyclops eat for dessert?

Eyes-cream.

When do zombies eat people?

On Chewsday.

What do sea monsters
have for lunch?

Fish and ships.

What did the zombie eat after the dentists pulled out all its teeth?

The dentist.

How does a polite monster greet you?

"Pleased to eat you!"

What did the Yeti eat for lunch?

An iceberger.

YUMMY!

GHOSTLY GIGGLES

Why did the phantom have such good hearing?

Because he was eerie.

What kind of mistakes do ghosts make?

Boo boos.

How do ghosts watch movies?

On a big-scream TV.

What is a pirate ghost's favorite color?

Navy boo.

What do baby ghosts wear on their feet?

Boo-ties.

What is a baby ghost's favorite color?

Baby boo.

18

When do ghosts wake up?

In the moaning.

What does Godzilla drive?

A monster truck.

TOO COOL!

What kind of monster is the best dancer?

The boogieman.

What is a monster's favorite treat?

Ghoul Scout cookies.

What is Bigfoot's favorite book?

Hairy Potter.

ACTIVITY: MONSTER MIX-UP

What you need:
- paper
- pencil
- markers, crayons, or colored pencils

What you do:
1. Create your own monster! Pick two monsters you like.
2. Combine their best features to make a new monster.
3. Color your monster and give it a name.
4. If you are feeling really creative, make up a joke to go with your new monster.

GLOSSARY

cyclops (SY-kops)—a monster with only one eye

eerie (EE-ree)—scary or creepy

haunted (HAWN-tid)—having mysterious events happen often, possibly due to visits from ghosts

phantom (FAN-tum)—another word for a ghost or spooky spirit

rotten (RAH-tun)—old and smelly, falling apart

READ MORE

Dahl, Michael. *Silly Jokes About Bugs*. North Mankato, MN: Capstone, 2020.

Elliott, Rob. *Laugh-Out-Loud Spooky Jokes for Kids*. New York: HarperCollins, 2016.

Pellowski, Michael J. *Mega-funny Jokes & Riddles*. New York: Sterling, 2017.

INTERNET SITES

Funology
www.funology.com/other-jokes-and-riddles

Kidactivities
kidactivities.net/halloween-jokes

INDEX